# Marked Men

*Also by Joseph Hutchison*

The Earth-Boat
Thread of the Real
Sentences
Greatest Hits 1970–2000
The Rain at Midnight
The Heart Inside the Heart
Bed of Coals
House of Mirrors
Sweet Nothing Noise
Wandering Music
The Undersides of Leaves
Thirst
Shadow-Light
Weathers, Vistas, Houses, Dust

# Marked Men

*Three Poems*
*by*
*Joseph Hutchison*

Turning Point Books

Published by Turning Point Books
P.O. Box 541106
Cincinnati, OH 45254-1106

ISBN: 978-1-62549-034-6
LCCN: 2013943790

Poetry Editor: Kevin Walzer
Business Editor: Lori Jareo

Visit us on the Web at www.turningpointbooks.com

*Acknowledgements*

The author thanks the editors of the publications in which
two of these poems first appeared:

*Divide Magazine:* "Colón in Extremis"
*Mad Blood:* "An Old Soldier of the Revolution"

Special thanks to the friends and fellow writers who read and
commented on "A Marked Man" during key stages of its
evolution—people without whom this poem would never
have found its true shape: Robert Cooperman, Dr. Michael
Hogan, Rita Brady Kiefer, David Mason, Joseph Nigg, Ed
McManis, Thomas R. Smith, and Sandra S. McRae. Special
thanks to Byron Strom, a relative of Silas Soule, who kindly
reviewed the manuscript and saved me from several historical
errors. Of course, all errors in the finished poem—both
historical and aesthetic—are my responsibility alone.

The epigraph to "A Marked Man" is from the essay "Fate,"
by Ralph Waldo Emerson, in *The Conduct of Life*, Volume VI
of *The Collected Works of Ralph Waldo Emerson* (Harvard
University Press, 2003).

The epigraph to "The Shuttered Heart" is from "The Poet's
Obligation" by Pablo Neruda (tr. Alastair Reid), in *The
Essential Neruda: Selected Poems* (City Lights Books, 2004).

# Table of Contents

*This Book Is for Melody*

# Marked Men

# I: Preludes

# Colón in Extremis

## I

The artist sits back, brush in hand, to take
his progress in. Yes, yes . . . the Great
Discoverer arches in his twisted
bedclothes as he must have; sweat
jewels the fleshy, whiskered jaw, slicks
the tangled hair made thin by grim ambition.
Do the eyes, rolled back in anguish, catch
more than the lamplight's soiled yellow glow?
The artist dips up a bit of pigment, daubs
at the inward corner of each eye—two ticks
of white. A magic touch! For suddenly
it feels as if Colón can see beyond the wall
on which his murdered Savior hangs,
beyond the Ocean Sea; it seems his vision's
found (at last) the gold-paved streets, walls
and roofs of gold that hover, shimmer, breathe
their whorish promises—toward which Colón's
whole body stretches, every muscle clenched,
each tendon taut . . . the succubine dream
wetting his mouth with its syphilitic kiss.
The artist smiles. It *works*. Especially
the way the hazy vista of Castile
outside the window seems to dwarf
Colón's death-throes. The season's Spring,
but the colors are impoverished—dusty blues,
bleached siennas, a greenishness suggesting
fields of stringy ryegrass, sullen reds.
One can almost hear the ill winds
keening through the clay-tiled belfry
of the Church of San Francisco (a spire
built of grays and browns, a shadowy slash,

a hint—no more, no less). The artist, deep
in hard thought, digs in his kinked beard,
pinches up a louse (fat with his own blood)
and crushes it on the edge of his palette:
another color he'll need to work in.

## II

She unglues one eye, then
    the other. Light
smears the cloud-tangled sky with a sheen
      like lanolined wool
    at shearing-time. She stretches, cattish,
slipping back the sheet
    so dawn can wash
the breast her last drunken lover slashed—
      the one he likes best
    (he'd spend an hour tonguing the scars
if she would let him.) There
    he is: turned
away, absorbed in colors, lines and shapes,
      shadows, dreams. Shouts
    bursting from the street don't seem
to touch him, nor the woven
    fragrances
of bakers' stalls, abattoirs, horse
      farts, the carcasses
    of pigeons crisping on spits—nor her
own sleep-thickened voice,
    it seems. She calls
again. He brandishes his brush, grunts
      good morning in that odd
    lilt. "You *twitter*," the old
man (drunk as ever)
    told him once.
"I almost hear those fire-plumed island birds
      you want to paint. *Do* it,
    then. *Annihilate* your palette!"
El Viejo's public likes
    his somber hues—
his purse is proof, although he never pays

for drinks and thinks the niñas
    should pay *him* (toward the end
of a night in the tavern he'll roar,
        "I'm an artist!
I've got a big *pija!*"——then stagger off,
        dragging smoke and laughter
    out into the night.
El Picante there has brushed
    his rowdy old
wicked mentor up from canvas voids
        half a dozen times——
    the only times his eye has touched
a subject lovingly,
    she thinks. Look
at the harsh light his savage heart's poured out
        over the dying man——
    Colón, he says, who hauled his father's
mother back to Spain
    from Paradise
in chains. She was, he claims, Taino ("A kind
        of monkey," the old man joked
    once behind his hand; he lost
a tooth when El Picante
    smashed his mouth).
From her he got his skin——whiskey brown,
        kid-glove smooth, though bleached
    a bit by Spanish blood. Her own
blood has been diluted too.
    So, at least,
her father thinks——he says it's why she fled
        a good sheep-herding life . . .
    for what? A life spent on her back?
It's not . . . I don't, she'd tried
    to tell him, heart
turning to lead in her chest. (It was the day

8

        they laid her mother down
    in the shadow of Mount Perdido.) Still,
she likes the feel of it,
    her painter's skin,
the taste of it—he tastes ... *exotic*. Look
        at those two long-boned arms,
    willowy wrists, the eyes that see
*through*, see *into* ... when
    they see. She frowns
at his back and snatches the wooden goblet up
        from the bedside box (a crate
    stood on end), raps it to knock
loose the roaches (two
    drop and scatter
like fire-shot cinders), and splashes into it
        the dregs of *tinto*: warm
    and dark and sour as her love.

## III

Hold the secondary figures back,
the old man says. The artist knows it: let
the context speak, the balance (or the lack
of it). And yet Colón's two sons resist—
sly Diego, craven Fernando . . . they kneel
beside the bed and claw the sheets, groan
their ostentatious prayers. They almost wreck
the composition, almost break the heart
of their creator—they who in life created
him, they and their brutal ilk . . . the scum
who split Taino women with their pricks,
Taino heads with swords, who killed for sport
the brilliant island birds and porpoises
and island children too, who worked to death
so many slaves, clawing up their gold
from the butchered earth. Hold back? he thinks.
Would Bosch hold back? But you're not *Bosch*, he hears
the old man croak, laugh sharp as a crow's. Christ,
in Spain you're barely a man. *Get used to it!*
The bastard's gruffness springs from fear: the whores
gossip that his manhood's hoodless, bald
whether soft or hard. *Circumcised,*
they whisper—meaning *Jew* (not that they care:
at least Jews pay; the Inquisition's spies
pay with blows, with threats): the old man dreams
of sword hilts knocking at his door in the dead
of night, of being dragged off in chains.
He also covets El Picante's Basque,
who poses nude for nothing more than meals,
a jug of wine, a laugh, a breathless roll
in the grass beside the Duero. And here she is,
a fragrant silence at his shoulder, wrapped
loosely in the sheet they tangled in

last night. "Look," he tells her, points his chin.
She's in the scene as well, as old Colón's
second wife, Beátriz. Leaning close
as if to sniff the paint, she says, "I see."
She's not impressed. She's been Athena, blithe
Aphrodite, nymphs and gypsy maids—
but here she's older, faded, grim-mouthed,
staring out a window with a look
of dim confusion. "What's that in my hand?"
she says. "The will." Colón, he tells her, left
Beátriz more than wealth—an insult,
an implication that she'd sold herself
while he was plying the Ocean Sea. "He left
her there to starve," he says. She nods, then shrugs.
"Hunger and morals seldom mix." He smiles.
"The old man says he'll be a saint one day."
"We live in crazy times," she laughs and leans
against him. Always a shock—her candid warmth.
He slides his hand inside the sheet, dips
a finger into her gently, like the tip
of a brush. "I need to get to work," he says.
She lets the sheet fall, breathing, "So you do."

IV

. . . and I burst in on them. No fault of my own! We've
been acquainted some years, he's learned a good deal
about art at my knee. And yes, as you've so *kindly* pointed
out, a bit about other sports as well. I admit it! Virtue's not
my strength. But God has granted me other talents. I've
painted courtiers, grandees, conquistadors fresh from the
New World and flush with riches. Even your Inquisitor has
sat for me! So you see—you see how your summons has
come at an opportune time. Yes, just yesterday I burst in
upon them, and the two of them—artist and model—
were engaged in a most . . . *un-Christian* act. But that's not
the worst of it. The worst of it is—his damned picture! A
slander on the man that first carried Christ to the Indies.
*Colón in Extremis*, he calls it. On the point of death he por-
trays him. Most piquantly, true—but truly to that great
man's disadvantage. To the disadvantage of all true
Spaniards! And the colors . . . *my* colors . . . though not in
service of their subject. Not for a patron's pleasure, I mean
. . . but for revenge. He bears great hatred for Colón. Be-
lieve me, I regret giving the poor ape such skills, not know-
ing how he'd misuse them. And truly, 'til I burst in on
them, I'd never noticed how *dusky* his complexion is. His
and his whore's both. Therefore I've only just come to
wonder, to suspect. Moorish blood? Or Jew? He calls him-
self *Taino*—not a Christian word, I think. But you're the
one who turns suspicion into proof. I trust your Superior
will find my help of value. *Muerto a los marranos!* As for me,
now I really must rush off to Mass—like my father before
me, and his father before him. . . .

## V

And when her screams subsided—
　　her cries to saints,
to Jesus and the Virgin (proof that she,
　　　　at least, was not a Jew
　　in secret, no?) . . . the torturers
stood back to view their work—
　　and he could see
from where he hung chained against the wall
　　　　just how it might be done—
　　how each lash of firelight,
each thread of blood, each tear,
　　the ember glow
of kilns and searing iron instruments,
　　　　the dog-like eagerness
　　of those who worked the tongs, the cool
patience of their Master—
　　how it all
might be rendered on a canvas, stroke
　　　　by stroke . . . or better, laid
　　down on weathered wood—a door
(let's say), set in some
　　public wall,
so people daily might pass and touch
　　　　the scene, marveling,
　　wondering what hand could shape
such a nightmare, what
　　nameless soul—
but then his head sank down, his bruised eyes
　　　　slowly blinking, breath
　　caught like a fat chunk of mutton
in his throat . . . until
　　his melting gaze
flowed down and touched the bloody worm,

      his sliced-off cock, thrown
    down on the straw——another color
he'll need to work in . . .

*Spanish Cross*
*Taino Sun Petroglyph*

# An Old Soldier of the Revolution
## *(Anno Domini 1801)*

You should of seen this district in the olden times, afore
    we cleared
the Iroquois out.
              *Oquaga*, they called it.
                              Forty-some houses
both sides the river. Chimneys, glass windows, trade-
    good crockery—
the people still brutes, though not a few called
    themselves Christians. They were
savages, in truth.

              They considered all this,
              far as the eye goes and more,
              their own. So when the Crocketts
              began selling tracts up Cherry Valley—
              where my own people went first,
              thanks to my Father's hoard
              of Spanish silver—the Iroquois
              started in killing settlers, those
              with deeds and those without.
              No respect for civilized contracts!
              About then General Washington
              was getting his army up
              to badger the King's soldiers
              back to England, and our bunch
              pretty quick got mustered
              into the Fourth Pennsylvania.
              The Iroquois misliked the Crocketts
              more than the British, and so
              became our bitter foes.
              Right here was our first skirmish.

We crept through that stand of trees there about dawn.
    A ways off—
not far from where we sit right now—we spied a young buck
        buck
leant up against his longhouse, answering the call.
    Colonel Butler
signaled us to halt and be quiet.
                    This was early October,
                        a month
of mild nights here. Scanty leaf-fall. Fat stars. Hoot-owls.
The moon shone like a whetted scythe blade. So quiet
you could hear at a hundred paces that red man's piss
sizzle in the dirt. Must of drank a barrel of English rum!
    Well,
Butler got a bit tetchy after a time, and made a circle
in the air with his fist, like this—and we cut loose,
swooped on the village, whooping and shooting.
                    Later,
me and Will Sweeney stumbled over that red bastard
face up in the mud, his eyes bald as spoons, fist
still gripped around his pizzle. Like to split
our sides laughing down at him, I swear.

That way, where the river bends—
not a few escaped that way. We could hear
paddles splashing between the *pop pop*
of our flintlocks.
          Sweeney picked off a girl—fifteen,
maybe—out to the middle there.
                Waist-up naked.
                  The shot
took one pap clean off, and over she went. The whole canoe
        canoe
went over, that girl and four more that looked younger.

But who can tell? Ever last one of 'em's red-brown and
     filthy,
horsetail hair stinking of bear grease and foul cook-
     smoke
and Lord knows what all.
                        Took us 'til mid-afternoon
to finish the job. We knocked down the longhouses, fired
the granaries—can't make war when you're starving!
Sweeney reckoned we torched some two thousand
     bushels.
A sweaty piece of work it was. Course,
it warn't all work. Toward sundown we had fun
wiping out the Oquaga cornfields.
                        Over there,
where you see our own crop's making now, Sweeney
and me and old Robert Gale—I say *old*
but he was young then, younger I bet than you (hell,
we was all young then:
                Frank Squires,
                Jesse Woods, that
                Cornelius What's-his-name
                    who became a parson:
I can see 'em like yesterday)—thirty or so patriots
mowing down the bone-dry stalks.
                     Now and then
we'd come across little ones their mothers
had tried to hide, froze up
like hairless rabbits in shallow
grass-strewn dugouts.
We'd stick 'em
and lift 'em up high
on our bayonets.
Hell of a thing—how
they'd twist and wiggle. . . .

19

Hey.
You all right?

Oh, no.
Don't tell me you
*feel* for 'em. . . .

Here now:
have yourself a swig of this,
straighten you right up.
Best liquor for miles around—
'cause the corn we make it from's Iroquois corn.
I swear, ain't nothin' sweeter this side of paradise.

*Flintlock*

*Iroquois Tomahawk*

II

# A Marked Man

> "If we must accept Fate, we are not less
> compelled to affirm liberty, the significance
> of the individual, the grandeur of duty,
> the power of character."
>
> —Emerson, *The Conduct of Life*

## I: A Damped-Down Fire

*April 21, 1865*
*Half Past 10:00 a.m.*

Boot-clatter out on the boardwalk's
warped pine planks—boisterous
shouts and catcalls that wrench his gaze
from the brew gone flat as pond water
in its thick-sided mug. Soule turns,
squints: the saloon door stands
open onto Larimer street, its mud
a slops-and-horseshit pudding
runny with April thaw. He leans
toward it, on alert, but doesn't rise,
merely gripping the glass mug-handle,
knuckles a sickly pinkish white.
Afraid? No man's stuck that slur
on him, nor he on himself. Still,
when he touches the dim star
pinned to his duster's black lapel,
its pointed reminder—Silas Soule,
Assistant Provost Marshal—his breath
stalls. Does he prod himself? Insist
that a brawl in the street's his bailiwick,
his duty (whatever *that* might mean
in times like these)? In any case,

the chair holds him fast.
                              Boylan,
the barkeep, dragging his twisted leg
like a cottonwood branch, eases
to the flyblown window for a peek
under the gilt-lettered words *Criterion
Saloon*, then shrugs toward the marshal.
Soule resumes the study of his lager.
Boylan takes up the damp rag tied
to his apron string and begins to wipe
the nearest table.
                    Two months it's been
since Soule testified—told the horrors
he'd seen at Sand Creek to the panel
convened by Colonel Moonlight.
A massacre, Soule called it, Chivington's
rubbing out of Black Kettle's village,
though some in Denver City said
we're at war, which made it a battle,
and some called Soule a damn traitor
because he kept his men above the fray.
Boylan has seen with his own eyes
how death threats have turned up
under Soule's plate while he stepped
out back for a piss. He eyes Soule now,
sidelong. Sure seems all the verve's
been bled right out of him—a man
that used to laugh at his own sly jokes,
or wax philosophical over losing
at cards.
          "It all evens out in the end,"
he'd say, then wink: "Dust to dust,
no matter you're planted with a jingle
in your pocket."
                  Of course, marriage

26

sobered him up. The very prospect
made him jump at the Colonel's offer
of a marshal's star and steady pay.
Then came the inquest, and fresh
strikes by the Arapaho and Cheyenne
hot to avenge Chivington's slaughter.
And Soule, for his testimony, called
by some an "Indian lover" like Tappan,
the man Moonlight picked to head
the investigation. *Small wonder*
*some hate him*, Boylan thinks. Still,
half the town feels damn appalled
by what was done, and looks on Soule
as a brave and honest man. Boylan
contemplates the marshal's contemplation.
Why don't he just *go on*? When Soule
sits down for a meal, the place
soon empties out—for who'd care
to risk their health by sitting near
so marked a man? Look at him. What
could he be reading in that spindly foam
scrawled across the pale gold surface
of his beer?

       Now a stamping of boots
brings some stranger in: battered valise
and derby, green paisley vest. Soule
doesn't stir as the man picks out a table
by the shrouded piano, swatting dust
from his trousers before taking a chair.
*This one's either unafraid*, thinks Boylan,
*or ignorant. Or both.* The new arrival
spots him and barks, "A Mule Skinner,
my good man."

       Boylan runs a thumbnail
across his whiskery chin, then drags

himself over to his customer. "Friend,
there's tequila in back, but I'm fresh out
of blackberry liquor."

The stranger's
brow wrinkles and he juts his jaw.
"What's *he* drinking?"

Boylan
can almost feel the marshal stiffen.
"Solomon Tascher," he says.

"Beer?"
the gent wonders.

"So-called,"
says Boylan.

The stranger shrugs.
"Beans and bacon too, if you got it—
and the bacon ain't rancid."

Boylan
grits his teeth. "That'll be three dollars,
friend. Gold only. Coin, or nuggets or dust
weighed at the bar."

The man frowns,
reaches inside his vest—and Boylan
blanches. But the fellow merely
brings forth a crooked black cheroot.
He holds it up with a kind of reverence,
like a golden nugget. "And a lucifer,
my man, if you got one."

"Sure thing,"
Boylan says, thinking, *And I ain't
your man.* He turns then to find
the marshal's up at last and headed
for the door.

"Take care now, Silas,"
he calls.

Without looking back,

Soule says, "G'day, John," and steps
out into the mild April sun.

"Here now,"
the gent says, a keenness in his voice.
"Would he be Captain Silas Soule?
Of Sand Creek?"

Boylan's eyes narrow.
"That's Silas Soule of Denver City,
Assistant Provost Marshal here.
Who wants to know?"

"Damn me,"
the man says. "He's what brought me
here from Boston."

Boylan hides a grin.
Had Soule heard that he'd crack, *Strange!*
*I'd have thought you'd traveled here*
*by stagecoach.*

"Boston," Boylan says.
His own home town.

"Boston, yes.
I write for *The Boston Journal.*"

"Do you, now?
You must know Perley, then. I used to read
his Washington Letters over breakfast, before
I lit out for the West."

"Perley," the man
drawls. "Sure. Hell of a pen."

Boylan
shrugs. "A good Whig," he said, "then
a good Republican. Like yourself,
I guess."

The man flashes a white smile.
"Sure," he says. "Of course."

"You're a bit
far from the Back Bay," Boylan says.

"Have you caught gold fever?"

                          "Not at all,"
the man laughs, then lowers his voice. "Y'see,
I'm here to follow the Sand Creek inquiry,
and interview the principals if I can."
He glances toward the window. Soule
stands outside with his back to the glass
like a man listening to distant thunder.
"Think he'd talk to me?"

                          This question
gives Boylan pause. Before Sand Creek,
before the inquest, Soule was the kind
you couldn't shut up. Now he smolders
like a damped-down fire. "Can't say,"
Boylan answers at last. "He's bound
for his office down the street, I believe.
I can't swear he'll be open to talk.
Could be he's talked enough."

## II: Lucky

*April 18, 1865*
*Morning*

Curious how her thoughts have drifted off, how dread
swept them into the middle distance like sparks of
    milkweed,
how they swirl among dust motes there, in a shaft of
    watery sunlight.

She glances down at the small book Silas gave her (it has
    closed on her finger),
and finds that her hand seems not to be hers, but a
    stranger's.

The dread and the dust and her whirling thoughts!

She grips the book to steady her. Green cloth, blind-
    stamped leaves and berries, the title a golden
    flourish.
It nestled, Silas told her, in one pocket or another of his
    duster from Boston to the gold-fevered camps of
    Denver City,
and from Denver City to his post at Fort Lyon and
    back—how many times in that grinding circuit?
How many stops at her family's ranch on Plum Creek,
    laying over at their Halfway House with his fellow
    Union soldiers,
before he noticed her, or allowed her to see he'd noticed?
    And then that night
in the hayloft above the chuffing horses and the milk
    cows' shuffling massiveness . . . *Is this then a touch?*
    *quivering me to a new identity. . .?* Her name
lost consciousness, she was no longer Hersa, nor

31

Coberly, but a firecoal he breathed on until she
flared and crumbled open. *The sentries*
*desert every other part of me—yes—they have left me helpless to*
*a red marauder.*
Sweet, sweet, sweet. . . .


And when the bands of Powderface and Whirlwind
shrilled out of the dry August dawn, one of a
dozen cattle raids that summer,
and her father raced shouting through the switchgrass
'til a feathered shaft sank its beak in his lung, and
he crumpled, gasping a bloody syrup over a tangle
of cholla,
how would she ever have outlived her grief if not for her
gentle Captain? Or expelled the moiling poison of
her hate?
"We've taken their land," he said simply, after the burial.
"They resist like cornered badgers, as we would
resist. As the Rebs are resisting. But Nature's law,"
Silas said, "is 'Change or die.' So the Indian will give in,
and General Lee will give in. And the land will
give up its gold."
He took a philosophical tone to calm her, she knew, but
something else hid under the words, sharp as a
sheathed knife.
He stroked her cheek. (In the parlor of Halfway House
they sat, the wainscoting daubed with colors from
the beveled window panes.)
"We ourselves must change," he whispered. His eyes
grew black, but seemed to blaze. "Be my wife," he
said.
And yes, she told him, yes, from Coberly to Soule I will
change.
I will change to mark what has already changed in me.

And though the Sand Creek horrors delayed it, and the
        want of a trusty income, they wedded the first day
        of April,
and for eighteen days she has been Hersa Soule. And
        during those days
Lee bowed to Grant in Virginia, and the actor Booth
        shot gaunt Lincoln dead, and threats of a like fate
have plagued her Silas with night-sweats, and dreams
        that drag him with garbled oaths and shouts into
        the shelter of her arms,
though in truth she can do nothing, and knows it and
        hates it.

Dread and dust and whirling thoughts . . .

Now she reopens the book, studies the engraving of its
        willowy author, the loose-fitting shirt open at the
        throat and tucked into plain laborer's trousers,
the black angled halo of his broad-brimmed hat, the
        trim beard black and gray, the eyes frank,
and turns the page to where Wendell Phillips inscribed
        the gift—"To My Dear Silas, Friend in the Cause,
        in Memory of John Brown"—
and from there finds her way back to the lines her
        thoughts had fled from.

*Has any one supposed it lucky to be born?*
*I hasten to inform him or her, it is just as lucky to die, and I*
        *know it.*

*III: Tidings*

*April 21, 1865*
*Approaching Noon*


Soule lays his pistol on the desk
between the *Cherry Creek Pioneer*
("Mourners of Lincoln to Pay Respects;
Funeral Train Reaches Baltimore
Today") and a letter sealed with wax.
He bites his flaring cigar
as smoke coils from a smile brought on
by the thought of leaving Boylan's Criterion

and hearing young Albert cry, "Marshal!
Hold up!" He gangled down the boardwalk
like a Spring calf and thumped to a halt
at his feet. His face was florid, sorely pocked
by the blight that had ravaged Annabelle,
his Mother. (Silas ached
to think of his first love in the grave.) Albert
panted, waving a square of paper. "The Major

told me to give you it." Silas grinned.
"You're a fine courier, Al," he said, and took
the letter. "I'll tell the Major you've done
a bully job." Digging into his pocket,
he withdrew a bright bronze coin.
"It's a two-cent piece. Look—
the first I've seen in Denver City."
Albert held it up and raptly studied

the shield with its waving ribbon that read,
*In God We Trust*. The verso showed a wreath
encircled by the words *United*

*States of America.* The boy breathed,
stammered, "Thank you, Sir," and bolted.
"Give your Pa my best!"
Silas called as Albert careered
off like a cowbird flushed from cover.

Soule lifts the message now, thumbs
the hard seal. Hesitates. *What
besides of sorrow, and dejection,
and despair, thy tidings bring.* Would
John Milton Chivington
know his namesake? Doubtful.
The Parson's a fighter, not a reader.
Silas snaps the seal, unfolds the letter:

five lines inked in Ned's elaborate hand.
*C. has dispatched a man. Maybe two.
Keep to your house and wife, my friend,
'til Tappan's work is done. I know
this won't sit well. You'll be inclined
to reject my counsel. Don't.*
Unsigned, which means he's serious.
But how surrender the street? Keep to his house

with no salary coming in? Now *that*
would be a pretty way to please a wife
and be seen as a coward to boot! And what—
leave Parson Chivington the last laugh?
Christ, the day before Colonel Moonlight
convened the commission (if
Ned recalls) the Parson whipped up his boys
with a sermon against "savages." "Five

hundred dollars for any good man that kills
an Indian or one of their sympathizers!" Now,

that last is Silas. Ned. Or their pal
Joe Cramer, or Cannon—that fellow
that joined in the mayhem but came to feel
its wrongness. Ned must know
it's half of the citizens in Denver City!
Are they all to cower like rabbits? All to flee?

At the door comes a sudden knock, and Soule
takes up his gun, pockets the note, swallows
dryly. "Who is it?" The voice is hale,
sanguine. "My name's Jack Dunn, Marshal.
A writer from Boston. Mister Boylan
said you might be partial
to an interview." Silas frowns, holsters
his pistol, and steps forward to open the door.

*IV: Ned Wynkoop to Kit Carson*

*April 19, 1865*

Greetings, Kit—and to your Josefina,
whose sweet reading voice, I know, will smooth
my roughest edges. I trust your return to Taos
inspired a parade of some kind. And now
it's rest you need. I hope you're right: I hope
the Army lets you turn it loose at last,
though how would they replace you? No one knows
as well as you the thousand natural shocks
these all but beaten tribes endure. I'm glad
you went to Washington, and spoke for them.
It's their respect that's keeping Taos safe,
that makes it home for you. Here—the raids
by certain bands of young Arapaho braves
have landed the city under martial law.
This has only made the dark mood darker.
It's all broils, betrayals, murderous plots—
and that's just the Whites! This Sand Creek
infamy has sent the lowest of the low
crawling the night streets with pig stickers
drawn, looking to slit a throat or two
in hopes of keeping the truth from coming out.
    Our friend Soule has borne the brunt of it.
After he mustered out, he found that no one,
not even supporters, would give him a bit of work
for fear of Thirdster retribution. Awhile
he champed the bit to try his luck back
in Kansas. Colonel Moonlight meant to help
and named him assistant provost marshal—
as which he's charged with getting cattle back
that Chivington's Third Regiment rogues
are pleased to steal and sell on the sly. Thus

he's widely hated amongst 'em. It rankles me
to hear him cursed at the Criterion Saloon
by men you wouldn't let pet your dog.

But seeing him not himself—there's the rub,
as the poet says. Where's the gregarious fellow
who used to sermonize back in Palmyra
at the Santa Fe Hotel of a Sunday morning,
now as a Methodist, now Baptist, now
a Transcendentalist of the Boston stripe,
each in succession and so persuasively
that all his listeners stood ready to swear
they'd gladly convert to each new Truth in turn?
Or the rascal that tricked the camp steward
out of a bottle of brandy—medicine for his pal,
Lieutenant Clark, who'd "fallen ill"—and got
the man to fill it twice by teasing a clutch
of flies into it and feigning an Irish outrage.
"Look! Is this the kind of brandy you dispense
to these poor sick soldiers here?" Waving
the fly-blown bottle like Patrick's staff.
The steward stammered his apologies
and sent Silas off with a fresh supply
of brandy for his men. That Irish gift
is why I brought him along to Camp Weld
with the Chiefs of the various Indian bands.
Sure enough, he read their mood and made them
trust the honesty of what I promised:
safety for their people, freedom enough
to hunt, freedom to sleep without fear,
all for settling down a while, some miles
from Fort Lyon, on Sand Creek. Evans,
our feckless Governor, attended, but deferred
to Chivington, all six-foot-seven of him,
all beard and glare and clipped dismissiveness.

"You say," the Parson told the Chiefs, "that peace

is what you long for. Well, peace depends
on your submission to military law."
He turned to me. "I leave this matter to you,
Major," he said, like some haughty king
handing his morning bedpan to a servant.
He ducked out the doorway then, Evans in tow.

    The Chiefs were flint-eyed, restive. Black Kettle
himself seemed struck by uncertainty. Soule
winked and shrugged and shook his head to show
he considered those other fellows crack-pated
preeners, while he and I were the ones that counted.

    We counted for nothing in the end, of course.
Chivington ignored our negotiations.
"I long to wade in gore," he said—a quip
over dinner at one of Evans' parties—
and followed with a discourse on the need
to wipe the Redskin from the Earth. "Root
and branch," he argued. "Men, women, babes
in arms—root and branch, I say." One guest
protested. "You're a man of God. Surely
God wouldn't have us butcher infants!"
Chivington bit down on a smile and snarled,
"Nits make lice." Yes. So far has the hero
fallen, the wily man who beat back Sibley's
Gray Coat Texans at Glorieta Pass,
who crushed Lee's dream of a sea to sea
Southland full of slaves. I've heard him
rail against the sinful trade in Blacks,
then from the same pulpit pray down ruin
on the Red Man. What's the true cause
he serves, I wonder. Soule thinks he knows.
"Once we're a state, Chivington wants a seat
in Congress," he told me once. Doubtless. Still,
ambition can't explain the order he barked
out on the ridge above the sleeping camp.

Of course I wasn't there. I was jolting
by horseback five hundred frigid miles
to Fort Riley, across the void of Kansas.
If General Curtis knew the situation,
knew the pledges we'd made at Fort Weld,
I felt he'd block action against the Cheyenne.
    But as I rode, the Parson rode. He led
the Third to Fort Lyon and sealed it off,
held the men loyal to me at gunpoint,
and two days later called the rest to stand
attention at his desk. These he knew
could not refuse: junior officers
like Joe Cramer, men like Soule (due
to muster out with nary a job in sight).
They would ride against the savages
and like it—so he said. Well, like it
they did not, but mounted up as ordered
and followed Chivington until, toward dawn,
they crested the ridge. The Parson turned to steel
in his saddle and spoke his will: "Kill them all!"
And that, Kit—that the Bloody Thirdsters
(so they're known in Denver) did with pleasure,
while Soule defied the order and held back
his men from joining that foul slaughter.
    My friend, I don't forget you know all this,
but garrulity—as you love to remind me—
is my favorite vice. To the point, then:
Soule's predicament is dire. I fear time
prepares a wicked fate for him. His life's
at risk, but years of soldiering, and some
rash investments in the fever dream
of gold, have left him with a purse as light
as when he first came West. My point is this:
Have you work for him? Or do you know
of any down your way? Denver City

is not safe. He must get out. You know
his mind is sharp, his heart loyal. I think
you know he's married now, settled down
with a bright, quiet girl named Hersa, one
of the Coberly clan. No more shenanigans
for him, my friend! I'll wager Silas Soule
could tame that sprawling ranch of yours, keep
the operation tight while you're off whipping
the spit out of the Kiowas and Apaches.
Those ranch hands that give you fits—soiled
doves and whiskey, sleeping off your profits
in the shade of some buffaloberry bush
while your cattle mosey the dry arroyos, prey
to rattlesnakes and Utes and what-all? Soule
could befriend their better angels, help them work
and savor honest toil for a change. And what
fine company Hersa Soule would make
for your dear Josefina. Civilize
the desert plains—that's my proposition!

    Well, as the Eternal Bard might say,
methinks I do cajole too much. Enough!
I haven't even asked how it feels to be
a brigadier general! Did the rank make
Mescalero bullets bounce off
your chest? It must have. Ever since we fought
together at Val Verde, success has dogged
your steps. You're passing into legend, Kit,
while I'm to take the Apollo stage again
in a month's time, reprising my famous role
as The Drunkard. Each to his own, it seems!
Write soon.
               Your faithful friend,
                    Ned

## V: The Conduct of Life

Here is the report I owe you, Parson.

Forgive its informality. I'm under the weather.

Let's be honest. I'm a bit drunk.

I interviewed Soule. We shared a flask but it wasn't enough.

Nobody told me, so it wasn't enough.

I rushed back to The Criterion afterward and drank the proprietor's rotgut, reading my notes over and over. Some clouds rolled up, then broke apart over the valley. I read at a table by the front window while the day brightened and dimmed.

My first notes are useless for your purpose. Common journalism—Soule is 26 years of age . . . Square jaw closely shaved . . . et cetera. Other irrelevant details I happen to like. Thus: Three books lay stacked on a pine crate behind his desk. A surveyor's handbook. A tattered volume on military law. Emerson's *The Conduct of Life*.

Nobody told me. I expected a frontier lout. . . .

He pointed to a chair across the desk from him, saying merely, "Mister Dunn." (I like that name Byers gave me. May use it again someday.) He kept his pistol holstered, but the holster clear of his coat.

I opened my notebook, mentioned *The Boston Journal*, as you instructed. He knew of it, and took the bait even quicker than Boylan. Who is this Perley? Boylan brought up the name and so did Soule. I had to repeat the lie that I knew him.

Soule said Major Tappan is nearly finished with him. Said soon enough Moonlight's Commission would publish the facts.

A profile is less about facts than character, I told him. Our readers hear of a White officer refusing to kill Indians, they want to know why.

I imagine they do, he said.

I told him I saw four possibilities, and ticked them off on one hand. Scruples. Misplaced affections. Disaffections of rank. And plain cowardice.

A flinty stare. This profile, he said, this canard of "character"—could it be meant to divert your readers from the facts of our life at war?

I expected some kind of bumpkin.

Let's see where the interview takes us, I said. Basics first. Your name is pronounced "Sole."

Yes.

Born 1838, state of Maine, city of Bath.

Yes.

Son of Amasa Soule, abolitionist and early member of the Emigrant Aid Society.

Yes. Son also of Sophia Soule.

Of course.

Mention her, if you would. I'd like her to see her name in print.

I'm told you once walked from Colorado to Kansas and back just to see her. In the dead of winter.

La Junta to Lawrence, he said. I know which friend you got that from.

I doubt that, sir. My sources are confidential.

I mean Mister Mash, he said. Sour Mash. And his eyes sparkled. I used to tell him all my secrets.

I couldn't help but laugh, but gathered my wits and pressed him about his father. The Emigrant Aid Society, I said. The aim of this group was to settle Kansas?

It was, he said. And to bring her into the Union as a free state. Which we did.

Rumor has it that your family homestead on Coal Creek, south of Lawrence, has served for years as a stop on the Underground Railroad.

He grinned. We'll have no need of that railroad now the South's been whipped.

Would the North go through with full emancipation, I asked, with Lincoln dead.

He gazed a moment out the office window. A view of snowy peaks some miles to the west. I think it unlikely, he said.

I confessed surprise at his pessimism.

He shrugged. North and South may settle, he said, but the war goes on in the West, and will—here and elsewhere, too. I fear the slave system will transform itself. I fear it will thrive in some new way.

What would your John Brown say to that? I said.

He is lucky to be in the grave, Soule said, without bitterness. He told me through the bars that America would see an orderly revolution. Orderly. . . .

Through the bars? I said.

After the insurrection at Harper's Ferry, when Brown was bound over for trial, a group of us saw a chance. I went to the Virginia prison one night and played drunk—gab and patter, stagger-dance, the whole bit of bloody Irish theater. They threw me in the cell next to Brown's for drying out. He knew my face and kept mum.

They say the man was insane. A mad fanatic.

*They* are almost never right, he said with a twisting smile. Brown lived in a dream, but the sanest dream I know. The freed negroes at Harper's Ferry would help their fellows rise up but not seek revenge. The worm-eaten tree of slavery, so firmly rooted in our Constitution, would simply crumble into its own hollowness. He believed his death would hasten that collapse—and so refused escape. He believed the revolution would spill little blood.

I couldn't help but mock him. What a farsighted man, I said.

Soule took the point and nodded. Brown never dreamed that some men love to kill, and find one cause as good as another.

You have some particular man in mind? I said.

I suggest you look into a gold-panner's eyes, he said. Examine the rapture there as he pores over the sand for glints. Listen to some booster touting the profits to be made from statehood. Watch the orator's fist quiver above his head as he calls on God to fulfill his own killing ambitions.

I did my duty and asked again whom he had in mind.

The war rages here, he said, and touched a finger briefly to his temple. Do you think it can ever end?

We sat silent awhile. That calls for a drink, I said and brought out my flask—just as I'm bringing it out now, as I write. (The bartender Boylan filled it before I came back to my room.)

Soule pulled two glasses from a drawer. We toasted Appomattox and drank.

I toast you too, Parson. And that little bag of gold you're holding for me. . . .

These notes have become hard to read. I've lit a candle against the waning light, and the flame's dance makes the brown scribbles writhe. Course, it could be Boylan's rotgut.

Let's consider more recent history, I said. Let's consider Chivington. A war hero, unlike Brown. A brilliant officer. A man of God.

Your terms! Soule said with a barking laugh. Your terms, and not a "fact" among 'em.

Well I asked for the facts then. He talked on and on—I have several pages here to prove it, though my hand cramped more than once. There are gaps, I mean. And much irrelevant to your purpose in any case.

Here it is in sum. . . .

On 27 November, Soule said, Lieutenant Cramer spotted fires from the tower at Fort Lyon and we rode out to investigate. Turned out to be Chivington's—a large camp. 700 of his Colorado Third Volunteers. Hundred Daysers, he said. You know the type?

I told him I did not.

Scofflaws, he said. Drunks. Down-at-the-heels miners busted by pyrite creeks. Runaways with ruined girls suffering back East in some poxy bed. Sharps with a scheme and a hidden knife. Such were the Parson's centurions, mustered against what he calls "the savage hordes."

Did he think them not savage? The degraded state of slaves, I said, is understandable. But these brutes seem to be savage by nature, not by subjection.

Soule fell quiet. When he spoke next his voice seemed compelled to obedience, like a high-strung horse in harness.

Let's consider savagery, he said. Chivington asked about the fort, did we have any Indians there. I said a few were camped at Sand Creek. "When he left for Kansas Major Wynkoop said they're to be considered prisoners of war," I said. A thought sparked in the Parson's eye, and I saw I'd blundered in mentioning the Major's absence. "We need to look into this," Chivington said. "Expect us this afternoon." Joe and I galloped back to the fort to alert Major Anthony, who quailed at the thought of upholding Wynkoop's orders. Sure enough, when Chivington rode in and set sentries up with instructions to let no one leave, Anthony said nothing—except to offer Chivington and his lieutenants a hot meal. At supper the Parson proceeded to browbeat us all about "consorting with the enemy." A few of us tried to talk sense, but Chivington cut us short with a glare. "Any man that helps the Indians is a traitor," he said, "pure and simple. And a candidate for hanging." This put Major Anthony in a terrible sweat, and over the next hours he stammered and groveled. In the end he surrendered the fort with nary a squeak.

Soule took up his glass and drained it.

So the Colonel countermanded the Major's order, I said. I thought the difference in rank spoke for itself.

The Colonel was no Colonel, he snapped. His enlistment expired two months before. He had no rank other than the one invented by Evans, no authority over the regular army—though Major Anthony was pleased to genuflect before him.

Soule's revelation disturbs me. It explains and supports his defiance.

But you're not concerned with my qualms, I'm sure.

Well, Soule spoke now as if he could see it all before him. We rode out sometime after midnight on the 29th, he said. Thirty below, the moon like a scythe. Our saddle gear made a crisp little music, and for some miles our horses' tails brushed the snow, 'til we came to a stretch where the wind had raked it thin. By the time we reached the ridge over Sand Creek our horses' muzzles were shagged with ice. The Parson signaled a halt. Dawn was creeping up over the camp. He made no pretense of fear.

He lined us up along the ridge in full sight of their look-outs. I think he hoped to incite a first shot from below, but no shot came, and soon he bristled, cursed under his breath—and finally gave the attack order. "Kill them all, big and little!" Afterwards, Byers' *Rocky Mountain News* quoted him saying he'd "loosed" us "like a flight of God's own arrows."

I couldn't help but laugh. I trust you'll take no offense.

Oh yes! Soule exlaimed with a grin. Chivington's half Agamemnon, half Jeremiah—*in his own mind*. It's a figure that goes down sweet amongst readers of Byers' scandal sheet. But it's an insult. A savagery. . . .

You felt *personally* insulted? I asked.

Soule shook his head. *Betrayed*, he said.

I wrote the word *betrayed* and paused. Soule sat in silence—as it were *in the grip* of that word—and his green eyes shone.

You see, he said, it was me at Camp Weld who backed up Major Wynkoop in his promises to the peace chiefs. Me. Now, you may have discerned that I have an Irish streak. I can spin a yarn, cadge a drink, dazzle a woman into bed (no longer, though—I'm gladly married). But when I give my true word I mean it. At Camp Weld I gave it. Straight from the heart.

And that's why you defied the order?

A company of men are an extension of their commander, he said. I could no more make them party to such betrayals than submit to them myself.

I asked him why he used the plural of that word.

Soule gazed out the window again as he spoke. The chief of the various groups at Sand Creek was Black Kettle, he said. One of the Camp Weld peace chiefs.

As the Parson's men rode down on the camp, Black Kettle stepped forth from his lodge and raised the Stars and Stripes on a rough-cut pole. We'd promised him . . . *I* had promised . . . that as long as that flag flew his people would be safe from harm. Black Kettle stood there with the confidence I'd sold him like a bottle of whiskey. Beside him his wisp of a wife stood with a white flag raised in a similar fashion. But neither symbol kept a clutch of Thirdsters from thundering up and unloading on the two of them point blank. They went down like sacks of dry beans. Did I take that personally? Oh yes. As if their guns were aimed at me.

Why did nobody tell me? I mean, the reports have been euphemistic, to say the least.

And here . . . here my notes give me pause. Not the wavering letters, but the substance. The writhing facts.

I fear you will not like them.

But your likes are not my business, are they?

So the nub of it is personal honor, I said.

He fixed me with a furious stare. Facts are not personal, he said. The impersonal facts are what betray us.

I asked for the facts, though I did not want them.

This time he did not look away. I saw a Thirdster hatchet a pregnant girl's arm clean off above the elbow, he said. Then split her head, and hack open her belly, and haul the infant out by its bloody cord.

He saw the heat rising into my face, but pressed on.

I saw fleeing children shot down like squirrels. I saw old men on their knees, resigning their throats to the sword. I saw one manly Thirdster leering over a dead squaw, whose dress was torn away—which inspired him to fish out his cock and piss onto her bush.

My thoughts swam. I felt ashamed. Though what

had all this to do with me?

There was a look on that soldier's face, Soule said, of *transport*.

Nobody told me. . . .

He sighed. Words aren't good for much when it comes to such things.

I wrote down *transport* nevertheless.

The last to die, he said, was the son of old John Smith, a White trapper whose wife was Cheyenne. The men who captured this half-breed boy meant to bundle him back to the fort, but the Parson found out and ordered no prisoners be taken. So the next day a man poked his pistol through a gap in the lodge where the boy was held and put a bullet in his head.

I took up the glass I'd poured for Soule and drained it myself—to little effect.

Would you not say we've all been betrayed? he said. As human creatures, I mean. Now there's a question for your thoughtful readers.

I told him yes—knowing, of course, that no one would ever inform "our readers."

Strange, he went on. What haunts me most are the things I didn't witness.

I don't understand, I said.

Some weeks after the massacre, he said, Chivington's men mounted a display of trophies at the Apollo Theatre. Scalps of children. Necklaces made of severed ears. So-called "tit-bags" made of skin peeled from the breasts of squaws. One fellow was proud to have killed Chief One Eye—our own hired spy, by the way!—and boasted how he sliced the man's scrotum off, stretched and dried it, and used it for a tobacco pouch.

50

A sickly quietness descended between us. I told him I had everything I needed, and thanked him.

This has been good for me, he said.
I asked him how so.
Our talk has made me of a mind to write it out, he said. My view of things. Facts of a kind Mr. Emerson, whose works I admire, would never sully a page with. And I believe this profile of yours could never include them. Yes?
I couldn't answer. My mouth was embittered by the taste of betrayal.
I thought not, he said.

We parted company in a low mood—which clings to me still.
You may understand why if you think back on the gelding of Chief One Eye.
Just know that by the time you read this I'll have placed a copy and the raw notes in a safe location, and left clear instructions with a man I trust, in the event something untoward befalls me.

But giving you this report gelds me, does it not. . . .

I'll need the payment agreed upon by 9 o'clock this evening. Your man can find me here at Eyser's Boarding House, unless I'm out on Blake Street taking the air. The foul miner-sweat and horse-fart air. . . .
May I say I can't wait for the morning stage? When I'm safely home, Parson, you·can count on seeing neither hide nor hair of me again.

Soule, of course, is another matter.

## VI: John Milton Chivington

*April 22, 1865*

The man's shaggy, brooding head
nimbused in a blue-gray smoke
slants like outcropped stone
over the desk's litter. A stub
cigar angles out of the cramped
mouth, each breath shaking loose
a snowfall of ash, each grunt,
each exasperated sigh. A narrow
window behind unfolds
a view of evening, the sun
gashed open on distant crags,
clouds like stained bandages
bannering over the dusk-flooded valley.
His thickset fingers flip the pages,
tug now at his beard's black scraggle, now
at an earlobe plump as a prickly pear.

Bastard, he thinks, and crushes
the rambling report in his fist.
Byers could do no better than
this sly wretch? Lily-livered
bleeding heart son of a bitch——. Well,
no matter. I am certainly confirmed
in what's been set in motion.
Righteous is as righteous does,
who am I to whistle back
the hounds? By tomorrow
this corrupt Commission will have lost
its most beguiling voice—this coward,
this insubordinate Soule.
Yet hearing Sand Creek
described in a courthouse atmosphere
does give pause. It sounds (strange
to say) wicked, although God
knows it cannot be. Elsewise
the Bible would say
*Thou Shalt Not Kill*
*Vermin.* It does not. It endows
Man with dominion over
Nature—cattle and cowbirds, deer, bears,
cutthoat trout, field mice, serpents—all!
Therefore these savages too. Odd
how these creatures' fates can so
move Christian folk
that they set aside
their rational fears to whine
about a few killed Indians.
Soule is why. Wynkoop,
yes—but he was absent
from the battlefield, and Soule
(they tell me) is better liked.
Soule is why. Soule is all that stands
between my blood-soaked past
and a fresh future
back in Washington.

He fishes a match out of his pocket,
strikes it, re-fires his cigar, lights the oil lamp's wick.
The westward range of mountains has blacked out. Night and cold
winds are bearing down on Denver City, on stables, barracks, churches, theaters,
poor miners' shacks and would-be mansions.
The War is over, he thinks. The Union saved. Soon its mighty feet will plunge
into both oceans. What sane man would refuse to accept the gift
God in his wisdom has laid before us?

## VII: Black Widow

*April 23, 1865*
*A Few Hours After Sundown*

A hand sets down a drink.
           Boylan's hand.
                       On the table
of rough-cut stone. The Criterion is all
           stone, not its daylight-
                       stained pine-wood.
                       The stone room
                       crowded
with shadowy figures, heads sheathed in black
           linen sacks. A whisper of
                       confiding
conversation, indistinct.
           "Drink up," says Boylan, voice
                 thick with
seeming sorrow. Soule drinks to soothe him.
           The whiskey's
                 color's wrong,
there's a biting smell—but down it goes
           in three long gulps.
                 At bottom,
a knot of
some kind of
darkness. Crushed
           spider. *Black Widow,*
                 he thinks. Boylan
flits away like a leaf in the wind,
           and a woman
                 glides out
from the back room, her face
           shrouded

                  like the others'. Soule
knows those scabbed hands, though—
          so he calls, but
                  the call
snags in his throat (a choking
          soundlessness. . .). Now
                  a tinny chiming
bursts from the sheeted piano,
          the vibrations
                  hollow as if
under water. Yet Annabelle's voice sparks
          upward with the clarity
                  of a cowbird's call:
"John Brown's body lies a mouldering
          in the grave . . ." And
                  from one stone table
two figures rise and rush toward him. *Hersa,*
          he cries (breathless,
          without sound),
          *dear God,*
                *Hersa,*

*help me. . . .*

## VIII: Small Gestures

*April 23, 1865*
*Half Past 9:00 p.m.*

She feigns sleep as Silas slips from their bed. He gropes
    about in the dark for his clothes,
and the windowed moon halos his nakedness, freshens
    her awareness of her own
breast buds touching their tips to the sheet, a sweet slow
    flash
like heat lightning under the skin, and something more,
    a tremor less benign,
as when out walking you feel suddenly observed—by
    hawk or serpent, Arapaho hunter or common
    thief—
so that your meander through knee-high switch grass
    seems perilous, though nothing
has changed, really: a mood, a dark whim is all. . . .

Is it that he cried out in a dream? That she held him
as he fiercely shivered and tore snatches of breath out of
    the dark, heart pounding?
And when he'd calmed down: "Just a nightmare, love.
    Just one of those falling dreams."

She watches him doubtfully as he half dresses, takes up
    his journal from the deal dresser, and slips away
    into the kitchen.
He eases himself into a chair at the table, scratches fire
    from a lucifer and lights a candle that puts out the
    moon, and leans into the glow, and begins to write.
His undershirt is red as ocotillo blossoms, the sleeves
    shrunk from too much washing, so that his wrists
    knob out below the cuffs.

How often she's kissed those wrists! The sparse red-gold
    hairs tickling her lips (she had not noticed a man's
    wrists before),
and she thinks she will never tire of them.
Now he pauses, and sitting back from the page draws a
    cheroot from a baking soda tin on the window sill
    and sets flame to the tip of it, puffing, making it
    flare,
then expertly shakes out the fire before the flame bites
    his finger.
The small gestures she has come to love. . . .

## IX: A Brawl in the Street

> *April 23, 1865*
> *A Quarter Past 10:00 p.m.*

A burst of shouts and hollers
startle his glance to the window
in the opposite wall. Too close.
Close by his own house. The chair
scrapes as Silas rises. He stubs
his fuming cheroot into the bent
tin ashtray, then grabs his gun belt
down from its hook.

"Silas!" Hersa calls from the bedroom,
a startled-from-sleep stridulation in her voice. "What's that ruckus?
Are you there, Silas?"

He steps toward her,
but halts just beyond the doorway.
She's up on one elbow, auburn hair
spilling over one smooth shoulder.
He'd forgot she fell asleep without
snugging back into her nightclothes.
And yet she looks summer-sultry
in the candle glow wavering in
from the kitchen. *This*, he thinks,
*this vision, is what I'll miss most
from the Earth.* "I'll be back, poppet,"
he blithely tells her. "Some miners
have got all roostered up, I'll bet.
Nothing to fret over."

"I can't help but fret, Silas.
With good reason." She pushes herself up to sitting, her small breasts
(two perfectly ripe peaches, Silas likes to say) made available to him
for a heartbeat or two, before she tucks them under the quilt edge
and clamps it tight with both bare arms.

58

                              "Luvver,
you don't play fair," Silas grins.
But it's pointless. She's in a pique.
"Listen," he says, coming close
and easing down onto the bed.
"I shouldn't have mentioned this
sickly feeling of mine. It's only
this blamed inquest. The curfew
doesn't help. The whole city's
on edge."
                 "You well know that feeling of yours
is more than a feeling," Hersa contends. "There are forces afoot.
And that Chivington—"
                        Outside, another blast
of whoops and curses, and a whack
like an ax handle striking a stump.
Then silence. Silas frowns. What
in the Sam Hill's happening?
                         "Those are not noises
a feeling makes, Silas. Those are *real*. Heed them. Attend to your inner
promptings. *You need not go.*"
                 Silas lets a long
slow breath puff out his cheeks,
then softly bites his lip, reaching
to stroke the olive skin of her arm
with the backs of his curled fingers,
shoulder to elbow, a silky warmth.
"You've been rattled by rumors,"
he mutters at last.
              Hersa shrugs his hand away
with a sullen laugh. "You must think me witless. When do I give a fig
for gossip? *Never* is when."
              "Still, it's in the air,"
Silas says. "And I fear my own
unease has made you fretful. This

is why I have to go. Duty, yes—
but there's some distress in my heart
that I have to subdue, or there'll never
be an end to it."
                    "Lord," Hersa grumbles, "I am sour
on this sorry subject."
                    "Ow! Ow! You devil!"
Then a noise of smashing glass.
                              "Go on," Hersa tells him.
"Duty calls." But her eyes are wet, her lips pressed thin. She is hugging
herself tightly, quaking.
                    Now a fresh flurry
of yelps in the night makes Silas
bolt up from the bed, a growl
ragged in his throat. "I am sick
to death of this hellabaloo!"
He snaps his black slouch hat
off the nearby chair's scrolled ear,
deliberately adjusts it onto his head.
"I *will* be back," he says, this time
to the wall.
                    Hersa watches him work his duster on,
a thin chill creeping from her stomach up into her chest as he moves
to the doorway. "Silas..."
                    He stops, steadies himself
against the jamb, then turns to Hersa
where she sits chin-deep in the shadow
his body casts across the bed. "Trust me,
poppet. This won't take long."
                    Hersa nods, offers
a tight smile. "Don't you forget what's under this quilt, Mister Soule—
and why it's here."
                    A surge of tenderness
swells his throat. "Never," he says.
Then turns again—but something

offhand Ned once told him
gives him pause: There's no
better target than a man's silhouette
in a lit doorway. Two long strides
take him to the table. He dabs
a forefinger and thumb
with the tip of his tongue,
pinches out the candle flame,
then eases toward the front door,
feeling his way forward in the dark.

## X: A Civilized Boy

April 26, 1865
Toward Noon

Mourners filing into the church    slow-moving figures
a rustle of crinolines    snatches of talk on the breeze
as when the boy wakes hearing leafy cottonwoods
close by the house in the dark    murmuring in some
secret tongue no human knows but the Red Man

    *Nature speaks to them*, Marshal Soule
        told him    *I saw an Arapaho hunter once*
    *kneel down by a snow-pool*    *and he spoke*
        *into an otter's ear*    *and by God that creature*
    *dove down*    *and in a blink swam back with a rainbow*
        *trout tight in his jaws*    *and me and that Indian*
    *dined quite nicely on it*, he said with a wink

The slow-moving mourners    mist away behind
his fish-bearing, Indian-loving-otter vision

    *Son! Rein him in, son*, the boy's father
        barks from the creek bank
    *You hear?*    *Albert?*

*I am*, the boy grouses    yanking the bit
hard against the mare's infamous skittishness

    *Sit tight*, his father orders

*Yessir*, says the boy    and looks down but watches
sidelong his father's cracked boots gouge the slick
Spring mud down to the water    and onward
into the gush and coil of it    making breath

catch under the boy's Sunday-best shirt
but his father doesn't falter    doesn't slip
on the smooth creek stones but with awkward
plunging high steps struggles across to the place
where his friend Major Wynkoop lay not far
from his horse

               (the hot-blood having panicked
at the crowd and reared    tossing him
down like a sack of seed beets)

                     the man
twisting as the boy's father stumbles near
and snatches up the dangling reins    now
patting the beast    making his famed
horse-soothing noises no doubt    each pat
sending puffs of dust up from the chestnut pelt

*Not "pelt"* the boy thinks    *the word's "coat"*

    How his mother would've laughed!
      *Oh, Albie*    then made him repeat
    *"Coat" not "pelt"*    before unraveling it
      for his edification    *"Pelt" is the hide*
  *off the beast*    lightly touching his cowlick
      *but on the beast you best say "coat"*
with that quick sunrise smile    and cheeks
    flushed he'd look off but hear her say
*Right words, Albie, are how folks know*
    *you're a civilized boy*    and then maybe
she'd send him outside with a fond look
    and a chunk of red rock candy

Now his father's helped the Major to his feet
and Albert winces at the way pain makes the man jerk
as if a Cheyenne arrow bit into the small of his back
the boy turns woozily away    finds the last mourners

clumping up the church's wide wooden steps

    Inside there'd be the Marshal laid out in a long box
      like the one they'd laid his mother in     the boy
    could still see the Marshal standing a long while
      beside it     looking down at the varnished floor)
    the memory makes him dig into his pocket    fish
      out the Marshal's coin and hold it up     sunlight
    glancing off it     glancing somehow into him
      calling up that time he was little    and he came
    limping barefoot into the house     a bee's stinger
      stabbing one heel like a rose thorn    but mother
    made a paste of baking soda and with her finger
      dabbed it on very gently so he wouldn't squirm
    'cause he hated tickling    though he'd suffer it now
      just to feel that feather-touch of hers again

Through tears he can make out his father splashing back
across the creek    and he clutches the coin and turns
to wipe his eyes with his sleeve    and when his father
takes the mare's reins Albert hears him mutter
under his breath, *Poor bastard*    with a solemn
shake of his head    then leads the mare in silence
to the tie-up east of the church and in silence ties her up

    *Here,* he says then    holding his arms up
      to lift Albert down    and hugs him awhile
    in silence    the one sound the fluttery rush
      of a cowbird swooping around the steeple
    veering crazily and piping as he flies

*Is he alright?* Albert murmurs into his father's
sweat-rich shoulder    *Mister Wynkoop?*

    His father sets him down carefully and nods

*You did good,* he whispers      then peers
at him inquiringly      but Albert's tongue
lays in his mouth like one of those
soggy-sticky wafers the priest feeds him
and at last his father gently drapes his arm
over his son's neck      *Hell of a day, Albie*
and glances up to where the cowbird
had been flying      but the air was empty now
*We best go in,* he says      *Your mother*
*would want us to pay our respects*

## XI: The Law Out West

*April 23, 1865*
*Half Past 10:00 p.m.*

The marshal forgot his marshal's star
    (it hung on the coat he'd put
on the bedroom hook), and out the door
    he bolted. Halted. Stood
still on the porch, touching his chest
where the star should be. —Well and good!
    A public man no more.

He could have gone back inside—but no.
    A voice barked out his name:
"Soule!" A graveled growl. "Hey, Soule!"
    From where? That narrow lane
to Cherry Creek, south and west,
or the rustling cottonwood that loomed
    northward from his house?

Fingers folding around the butt
    of his holstered Colt, he hopped
down into the thick spring mud
    and took some awkward steps.
A cold wind gusted over the crest
of the eastward hill; the marshal stooped
    into the thrust of it.

Against the stars like fields of grain
    the moon's sickle gleamed.
The night breeze carried a scent of rain.
    A far-off cloud bank dreamed
a dream of shattered light, expressed
in thunder the same dread that seemed

to grumble in his brain.

The ground sucked at his worn brogans
    as he passed some Sibley tents
where no lamps shone—a dozen,
      maybe more. Where were the men
who wasted their lives raking dust
for glints, the doves who kissed their senses
    to sleep at each day's end?

As if in answer a voice lazed out
    from among the tents somewhere.
"Ah we lahst, Captain?" A stout
    Virginia drawl—familiar,
somehow. "Friend, I'm *never* lost,"
he called, "but *you* may be. Come here
    and tell me what you're about."

Now a cloud swallowed the moon,
    made the air a black
shifting veil. His drew his gun,
    aimed it tentward, cocked
the hammer and cried: "Show your face!"
He caught no sight of the man at his back
    until the flash of a swung

axe handle smashed his wrist,
    then his jaw. The gun
thumped down as Silas twisted,
    staggered, slumping as he clung
to his attacker's sheepskin vest.
"Hey!" The man's breath stung.
    "Lemme go, ya shit!"

The second man sauntered up.

"Billy . . . be kind," he ordered
softly. "Captain, you look whipped."
    The marshal sagged, mustered
enough strength not to fall. His crushed
wrist screamed as they heaved and bantered,
        until they'd propped him up.

The clouds cracked open then, a flood
        of moonlight leaking through.
They turned the marshal loose. He stood
        staring at them. "You,"
he said to the one who stank. "I guess
we've met. I seem to recall you, soaked
        in a Cheyenne baby's blood."

"Bloody and proud," he said. "But Soule——
        you wouldn't know about pride
now, would ya?" "Nor loyalty, Bill,"
        the other said. Bill eyed
the marshal, nodded and spat. "We best
get this ovah," the other man said.
        "I fear I'll catch a chill."

The marshal studied him. "Squires?"
        The man shammed a salute.
Now Silas groaned: a rusty wire
        was being drawn through
his body, wrist to skull—then a blast
of cramping pain. "You won't shoot,"
        the marshal gasped. "Liar,"

Squires laughed. "I *saw*," the marshal
        hissed. "You liked the knife.
You liked the unarmed girls. Well,
        I know your ilk." "And I

yours," Squires snapped. "All this"—
he flung his burly arms out wide—
    "you'd let it go to hell!

Our work. Our wealth. Our *dreams*." He drew
    his pistol. Silas slurred,
"So Denver's law tonight is *you?*"
    "The *law*," said Squires. "It's but a word.
I'd love to erase the law out West."
Behind Silas's eyes, a roar
    of thorny light: "So do

what you will." Squires' shot
    shattered the marshal's head,
crumpled him back. His slathered hat
    steamed in the clotted mud.
The killers fled then, racing past
the house where Hersa leaned in bed,
    shivering under the coverlet.

## XII: Mount Prospect Cemetery

*March 23, 1893*


Hard to credit the size of the stacked coffins—
three foot by two by eighteen inches deep.
                                 Thus
can all the corpses in the city's potter's field
be broken to fit
                   and carted five miles
north to Riverside, for interment
                              en masse.
The *Rocky Mountain Herald* calls it "ghoulish,"
but the city pays under two dollars a box—
a price the mayor can crow about
come the next election.
                     Albert looks away
from the shoveling dollar-a-dayers. His gaze
drifts with the late winter morning mist
over Mount Prospect gone to ruin—the once
neat grounds given over
                       to thistle, bunchgrass,
prickly pear. Stones of even the wealthy dead
stand
        cracked, askew, lay
                     shattered to rubble
by vandals, and the wrought iron fence
collapsed.
        A damn shame.
               Now Albert
makes his way back upslope and eastward. Off
to his left,
           scrawny men in the Chinese section
toil to extract their own,
                 just as a somber group

of Jews in the Hebrew section do, downhill
to his right.

        The section Albert walks
had early on been Federal land, set aside
for soldiers. Then some clerk in Washington
discovered the deed had been hack work
by some crapulous factotum sloshing
through a life of patronage. Months later,
Congress conveyed the land back to the city;
but the city disliked the upkeep of all
those graves.

        Therefore, the local leaders
declared the site a future public park, ordered
families of the dead to unbury their forebears
and plant them

        elsewhere—at their own
expense, naturally.

        Albert himself had ached
his way through his parents' removal—
though he secretly admits preferring the view
at Riverside,

        the Platte roiling by in spring,
in summer gliding by,

        the Rockies lofted blue
to the west, the peaks and streaming clouds
purple and rose at sunset. . . .

        *The dead
here*, he thinks, *the Army will take care of.
A sacred trust.*

        Yet here he is—the overseer!
And why?

        All thanks to a knock last week
at his office door—not loud, but imperative.
He opened it to find a sixty-something fellow
with silver hair and silver beard, heavy-lidded

eyes, and a smile both shy and firm.

He said,
"You may not remember me. Sam Tappan.
I knew your father."

"By God," said Albert,
and took Tappan's hand. "Of course. You led
Moonlight's Sand Creek Commission. Come in,
come in."

Albert noted the older man's limp,
and so stood near him as he eased into one of his
Golden Oak chairs, then poured them each a sherry.
"I'm obliged," said Tappan. "My Cora won't allow
me spirits—except, of course, those that come
from that place beyond."

Albert forced a smile.
The news he'd had of Cora Tappan, *née* Scott,
disturbed him: her trances on stage, her so-called
"spiritual eloquence."

*Place beyond indeed*,
he thought, but said only, "I did hear you live
in Washington now."

"So we do," Tappan said,
"though this business of Chivington's claim
of $30,000 against the Sioux for horse stealing
brings me to Denver now and then." His hand
made a fishlike gesture. "Wending its way,"
he laughed.

Albert smiled faintly. "The law
is nothing if not deliberate. You're here
for that fiasco then?"

Tappan looked down
into his glass. "I'm here just briefly. To see you."
He looked Albert in the eyes as he took a sip.
"And what do I find? Not Albie, but his father—
the very spit! You do him proud, I see."

                                        "Well,"
Albert said, "he used to tell me, 'Undertakers
and lawyers, son. Even middling, they don't
go hungry.' So here I am."
                        "And here am I,"
Tappan said, then went on to confide he'd heard
rumors of men still loyal to the Parson—men
who meant to turn the disorder at Mount Prospect
to his advantage somehow. "They aim," he said,
"to steal Soule's remains."
                        "What on Earth?"
Albert asked.
                        Tappan shrugged. "I shudder
to guess. Some public desecration. Or leverage
for the old man's claim, perhaps. In any case,
some of us hope you'll bring your own good will
to bear. We'll pay you well to secure the grave
and supervise Soule's removal."
                        "Mister Tappan,"
Albert drawled, "I handle water rights, is all.
Not security."
                        "You knew him."
                                        "Thirty years
back," he said. "I was a child."
                        Tappan's look
scalded. "Soule was good to you. A friend
to both your parents." His jaw-muscle throbbed.
"Are there statutes of limitations now on debts
of kindness?"
                        Albert looked away, but couldn't
avoid the glass-doored bookcase against the wall
behind his guest—the shelf where he could see
that book received on his eleventh birthday,
a gift from the widow Soule: *The Conduct of Life*.
The card in it he had by heart. *My husband*

*would want you to have this, Albert. He cared
for you more than you know.* "I don't know,"
Albert muttered.

        "Think it over," said Tappan.
"Your mother——"

          "Fine!" Albert cut him off.
"No more  I'll take it on," he said.

              Thus
does Albert Coyle, attorney at law, find himself
the employer of two hired men eking their way
into the damp prairie soil—not for gold,
but bones.

        In fact, he's just back from his stroll
when the man called Clarence startles upright,
waist deep in the crumbling hole.

          "What is it?"
Albert says, crouching.

          Clarence glances up,
stabs with his shovel: a hollow thunk. "I think
we're home," he says, eyeing his fellow digger.
"Say what, Oscar—an hour?"

           "Figger two,"
the man replies.

        "Whatever you need,"
Albert mutters, gazing down not at the men,
but into the Earth—as if it were a rocking cradle
where no child lay, but a kind

              of changeling.
He straightens. "Do your job. I'll wait
over in the Phaeton."

          He turns, unsteadily,
as if a great boulder's balanced on his back,
and walks to the buggy where the docile mare
stands in harness. He's parked the buckboard
close by, with the sleek new coffin in back

that Tappan's man brought the day before.
Beside it,
        the salvaged gravestone.
                        Albert
contemplates the narrow, mottled marble slab,
the etched chevron and Army boilerplate:
        S S SOULE
        CAPT CO D
        1 COLORADO CAV
and underneath, the bald salient dates:
        1838
        1865
Now Albert scrambles up into the wagon.
The handsome coffin has a burnish so fine
he can see himself in it.
                He lifts the lid's
thickness, studies
           the canopy's pearl gray
satin sky, the pearly satin
              of the bed, the pillow's
immaculate sheen . . .
         *dear God*—
              his mind
all of a sudden empties into the box like wind
whirling down a canyon. . . .
             He digs his fingers
into his vest now,
        finds and unpockets
the bronze two-cent piece Soule gave him
that Friday of his last week on Earth, and tucks it
under the glossy pillow, and creaks the lid down
on a soft thud.
        Moments later, in the buggy,
Albert recalls his hand taking Tappan's elbow
at the office door.

   "Tell me, sir. Did Soule
love my mother? Did she spurn him?
Or did he spurn her?"

     "This is why Cora
keeps me from the likes of that sherry,"
Tappan said. "It inspires such daft thoughts
in men like us."

    He pressed Albert's arm,
then turned to limp away down the unlit hall.

## XIII: The Cowbird

*April 26, 1865—*
*and this very moment*

We've awakened in motion. Our shoes scuff the Earth.
We've awakened as members of the somber procession.

Black the caisson that jounces and creaks,
the geldings black, and their tack, and the funeral
    plumes
atop their heads sway like poplars charcoaled on a
    pristine pre-dawn sky.

A chill breeze licks into our sleeves; the afternoon sun's
    too April-weak to warm us.

We're crossing the cleared prairie east of Saint John's
    Church in the Wilderness.
How sweet-strange to remember the later St. John's (the
    cathedral of soaring
interior marble, those sinewy arches), the granite façade
    of it already there
in the future as we move across the prairie, Reverend
    Hitchings' eulogy fresh
in our heads, and the clear *hubbub-tseee* of a cowbird up
    in the belfry as he spoke:

> *Did he not in the darkness of the night*
> *go out to discharge his duty as commander*
> *of the Provost Guard of this city? Did he not*
> *go when he had every reason to believe*
> *that the alarm which called him out*
> *was only to decoy him into danger? There*
> *is the spirit of the soldier.*

We walk the dirt streets among pine-barked log cabins,
    newer homes and storefronts
of whitewashed wood, here and there brick warehouses
    and public buildings.
Farther on we pass among tall Sibleys and smaller wedge
    tents
where greed-addled miners nurse their dreams and kiss
    the pouty mouths
of whiskey bottles. Grizzled heads bow as we pass, out of
    affection for the Law,
and a brown-cowled cowbird—the belfry bird or one of
    his cousins—darts
from tent to tent, his wings and body flashing black. At
    each perch a *hubbub-tseee*
splits his beak, and he quickens into a crazed flutter-
    dance.

> The cowbird lacks
>     the owl's clairvoyance.
> The dove is more tireless,
>     the crow more resourceful.
> Unlike the hoopoe,
>     the cowbird's no mystic.
> He leaves eagles to haunt the crags,
>     lets the nightingale charm.
> The cowbird
>     is not the phoenix:
> one day he flits into the brush
>     and dies alone; doesn't return,
> but lends his intricate song
>     to the next cowbird—
> a song that reaches
>     back all the way
> to our first days on Earth.

With the cowbird's descant, the color of beginnings, we
    ascend Mount Prospect
with others who cared for the man in the caisson. Two
    hundred soldiers and citizens
of the city's five thousand, wending and climbing, silent
    and murmuring together.

There's John Boylan dragging his dead-weight leg,
fleshy nose red from weeping or whiskey or both.
    May the cowbird sing him a dream of dancing
past pain.

    There's Ned Wynkoop, who gingerly leans in the
saddle (the pain with its roots twined about his kidneys is
only now unfolding in his candid face
        its flower of chalk).
    May the cowbird sing a quarter century from
now, when that good man dies in Santa Fe, the long
thorns of Bright's Disease stabbing inside him.

    There's Aaron Coyle with his young son Albert
riding tandem,
    and Major Samuel Tappan erect in the saddle,
grim-jawed and eyes glinting like sword-tips, and
Colonel Moonlight riding lost in thought beside him,
    and behind them young George Ruter, the
provost guard who found Soule's body,
    and Doctor William Cunningham, who struggled
to treat Soule's mortal wound,
    and Lieutenant Jim Cannon, who in a few weeks
will apprehend the killer Charles Squires in New Mexico
and drag him back to Denver for trial, only to see him
escape, and himself weeks later suffer death at the hands
of a furtive poisoner.
    May choirs of cowbirds sing their spirits to rest!

And here, behind the caisson, Hersa comes
clutching her brother William's arm at the elbow,
walking (she insisted on it) without seeming effort,
stiffened by grief inside the crisp black crinoline of her
mourning dress. It is luckier to die, she must think,
    or we must think for her, as we move
    among shimmering ghosts of Gilded Age
gingerbread homes. and red brick late Victorians, and
tall half-glass luxury apartments from the Greed-is-Good
1980s, the grassy expanse of Cheesman Park and the
Botanic Gardens farther on
    misting into view and then dissolving,
    leaving us here with Hersa at the grave dug into
the prairie, and the others have departed,
    a jaundiced storm-light pours down from thick
Spring clouds, but she hesitates to leave,
    she has laid her husband's silver star on his stone
and studies it,
    we study it with her,
    its detached irrelevance—or its shining relevance,
a salvaged meaning, a justification,
    we are here
    but must admit she is unknown to us, is perhaps
already preparing her death
    in fourteen years, after remarriage and children,
feeling perhaps in the faint wind the chill of her own
future grave not far (in the end) from Silas at Riverside,
    we know her future is there and yet uncertain,
    nothing at this moment is written,
    she is in this moment and therefore free,
    free of her youth and her wifeliness, free even of
this dream we dream of her.

There is nothing but storm-light now, and the shadowed
    mountains, chilly wind gusts

crying over the incised stone. Now Hersa bends down to
      retrieve the marshal's star,
and with a distance in her glance (she has looked our
      way, for a moment
may fancy she can see us, see something, or maybe
      nothing, maybe only the breath
of timeless time), she pins the star to the black silk of her
      bodice, her fingers tremble as she
pins it, spilling spangles of storm-light on the sandy
      ground. We ache to call her name,
but in truth we have no voice here, and so simply join
      her in listening. . . .

> Wind groans overhead.
>    Small bees drone
> in a purple spray of larkspur.
>    A cowbird shrills—
> *hubbub-tseee!*—from
>    the black wrought-iron
> of the graveyard gate.

*Afterword*

# Shuttered Hearts

"So, through me, freedom and the sea
will make their answer to the shuttered heart."

—Pablo Neruda, "The Poet's Obligation"

Poems on historical subjects must be based on some sort of authentic connection to what happened, though they are mercifully less restricted in their handling of what happened than historical novels or histories proper. This is why readers may need a bit of orientation to the historical realities underlying the poems that follow. My obligation has been to historical essences as I understand them, not to the forms required by Realism or the documentary facts historians rightly value.

The deep background of all these poems is the European Conquest of the Americas, which began when Christopher Columbus stumbled onto the island of Bermuda in 1492. It is a history shaped by what Neruda would call "shuttered hearts."

Back in Spain, the Inquisition—a Christian Church-backed secret police force that sought to erase non-Christians from majority Christian nations—was in full swing. Spanish Jews and the last of the Muslim Moors had recently been expelled, which freed the Inquisition to focus on *conversos*—Jews, mostly, who had insincerely converted to Christianity in order to avoid various forms of legalized oppression. The Inquisition routinely imprisoned and tortured *conversos* to force confessions, killing and maiming thousands in the process. Survivors typically saw their property seized and divided between the Church and the state.

*Conversos* were popularly known as *Marranos*, a

Spanish word meaning both "pigs" and "unprincipled men" (a term still used by the *Catholic Encyclopedia*). This label doubtless helped to dehumanize these individuals enough to ease the conscience of their Christian torturers, as similar dehumanizing labels help to ease the conscience of torturers today.

In any event, Columbus in the New World proved to be a perfect expression of both the Inquisition's fanatical piety and the government's greed. He quickly established some core values that shaped the Conquest as it progressed over the next 400 years:

- A right of European ownership wherever Europeans happened to set foot;
- Automatic authority over any peoples the Europeans encountered;
- An assumption that being white and Christian conferred mental and moral superiority; and
- An inherent right to deprive the indigenous population of property, liberty, life, and whatever forms of wealth their lands and labor might yield.

All of these values were fostered by Columbus's belief in a "universal" religion and were later secularized, in the United States, in the concept of Manifest Destiny.

The arc described by the poems gathered here begins with Columbus and ends in the American West today—a "today" that in some sense exists outside of time, although in the poem it also coexists with the Civil War and the genocide perpetrated upon Native Americans that preceded and followed our fratricidal conflict. The arc is sketched in two "preludes" and arrives at our doorstep in the form of the book's longest poem.

The most helpful way to put all this in context is simply to follow that arc.

"Colón in Extremis," the first of the preludes, is set several years after the death of Columbus, who expired on May 20, 1506. The poem was inspired by a sentence or two in Kirkpatrick Sale's *The Conquest of Paradise: Christopher Columbus and the Columbian Legacy*. Sale notes that Columbus ended his first voyage by returning to Spain with a small group of captive Taínos (a sea-faring subgroup of the Arawak, the indigenous peoples of the Greater Antilles and South America). Sale doesn't say what became of the Taíno captives, and because the imagination abhors a vacuum, mine rushed in.

I imagined he must have presented them at the court of Ferdinand and Isabella, and based on the harsh treatment Columbus received later, I assumed the monarchs didn't find them a fit substitute for gold. History tells us that European men are attracted to "natural" (i.e., indigenous) women, so I assumed that after their turn at court the Taíno women in Columbus's party suffered the usual fate.

In any event, my biracial artist-hero is the product of such a union. The betrayal that ultimately places him in the hands of the Inquisition won't surprise anyone familiar with the way police states operate.

I felt compelled to write the second prelude, "An Old Soldier of the Revolution," after reading the chapter entitled "Oquaga: Dissension and Destruction on the Susquehanna" in Colin G. Calloway's *The American Revolution in Indian Country: Crisis and Diversity in Native American Communities*. American Continental Army forces destroyed this Iroquois town in early October 1788. The poem's speaker, a veteran of that action, recounts it some 13 years later. I imagine him as having been a member of the New York militia that fought alongside the Army regulars, since at the time the poem takes place he owns some of the land where Oquaga stood. Several lines in his monologue are taken almost verbatim from statements by various veterans of the campaign, as quoted by Calloway.

"A Marked Man" is set primarily on the day in 1865 when the Provost Marshal of Denver (then Denver City, Territory of Colorado) was gunned down by two assassins.

The marshal was Silas Soule, a former Army Captain who had refused to let his men participate in the massacre of old men, women, and children in a peaceable Cheyenne Indian camp on the banks of Sand Creek in the east central part of the Territory. The man who led the assault at Sand Creek was Colonel J. M. Chivington, who appears in the present of the poem only once but whose presence haunts the whole of it. In the wake of the massacre, a federal inquiry was mounted to look into Chivington's actions, and in those proceedings Soule testified against him.

There is no direct evidence that Chivington arranged for Silas Soule's murder, and it may be that a couple of his supporters simply got carried away, inspired perhaps by the assassination of President Lincoln a week or so earlier. In my view it scarcely matters. It was the mentality that the Protestant Chivington had inherited from the pre-Reformation Christian Columbus that killed Silas Soule, whose spirit of humane tolerance could not survive the forces of dehumanizing fanaticism.

Whether that spirit will survive and even flourish in the future, no one knows. But we're entitled to hope that shuttered hearts may open at last.

—

CPSIA information can be obtained at www.ICGtesting.com
Printed in the USA
BVOW05s1138301115

428844BV00001B/85/P

9 781625 490346